D0116003

PARRAGON

THE FLOWER GARDEN

LANCE HATTATT

Illustrations by
ELAINE FRANKS

This edition first published in 1997 by
Parragon
Units 13–17 Avonbridge Trading Estate
Atlantic Road, Avonmouth
Bristol BS11 9QD

Produced by
Robert Ditchfield Publishers

Text and artwork copyright © Parragon 1996
Photographs copyright © Robert Ditchfield Ltd 1996
This edition copyright © Parragon 1997

This book is sold subject to the condition that it shall not,
by way of trade or otherwise, be lent, resold, hired out or
otherwise circulated without the publisher's prior consent in
any form of binding or cover than that in which it is
published and without similar condition being imposed on
the subsequent purchaser.

ISBN 0 75252 140 3

A copy of the British Library Cataloguing in Publication
Data is available from the Library.

Typeset by Action Typesetting Ltd, Gloucester
Colour origination by Colour Quest Graphic Services Ltd,
London E9
Printed and bound in Italy

"With thanks to **J**"

SYMBOLS

Where measurements are given, the first is the plant's height
followed by its spread.
The following symbols are also used in this book:
  ○ = thrives best or only in full sun
  ◑ = thrives best or only in part-shade
  ● = succeeds in full shade
  E = evergreen
Where no sun symbol and no reference to sun or shade is
made in the text, it can be assumed that the plant tolerates
sun or light shade.

POISONOUS PLANTS

Many plants are poisonous and it must be assumed that no
part of a plant should be eaten unless it is known that it is
edible.

CONTENTS

THE FLOWER GARDEN

Everyone loves a flower garden. For it is here that a multitude of delightful and lovely plants can be brought together into a picturesque whole. The combining of colour, the consideration of form and the appreciation of texture will all contribute to harmonious and pleasing flower borders.

POSITIONING PLANTS

Border preparation is essential if flowering plants are to perform well. Following the removal of all perennial weeds and coarse grasses, the ground should be well dug to incorporate plenty of organic matter. Heavy or poorly drained soil may be improved by the addition of well rotted compost, sharp sand, bonfire ash or horticultural grit.

Container-grown plants allow planting at virtually any time although extremes of weather should be avoided. It is worth taking trouble when planting to give plants the best possible start. For this a good-sized hole needs to be dug to which should be added mature compost. Once removed from their pots, plants should be placed to a depth which corresponds with the original soil mark. Where a strong root system exists, roots may be gently teased out before filling in the hole and firming round to eliminate any air pockets. A thorough watering should then be given.

The way in which a border faces, the aspect, and the amount of sun or shade it receives has a bearing on what will grow. An open, sunny site with some shelter at the rear is ideal for many sun-loving plants. Shade, cast by a canopy of tree leaves, prevents certain plants from flourishing.

Opposite: This is very confident use of colour.

In cool, moist part-shade, *Primula florindae* (Giant cowslip)
rises above orange mimulus.

The degree of alkalinity or acidity of the soil,
measured on a pH scale, determines what will
thrive. A pH of 7.0 indicates a neutral soil, above is
alkaline, below acid. Some plants will not tolerate
lime and will only succeed on acid soils with a low
pH. Others demand more alkaline conditions.

THE FLOWERS

Mixing together annuals, biennials, perennials and
bulbs in the flower borders will give colour and
interest for the greater part of the year.

A hardy annual completes its life cycle in one year.
Grown from seed it will germinate, flower, set seed
and die within a single season. Seeds are usually
sown in the open ground in the spring. Half-hardy

Lilium 'King Pete', a robust low-growing lily, flowers in mid-summer.

annuals behave in exactly the same manner but the seed needs to be sown under cover. Young plants are set out when the threat of frosts is past.

In contrast a biennial requires two seasons. During the first it will produce stems and leaves, delaying flowering until the second when it too will set seed and die.

Perennial plants will establish and remain in the border for a number of years. As a general rule they make new growth in the spring, flower, then die down in the winter. Not all are totally hardy and some may not survive severe weather Others are evergreen and so do not completely disappear.

Bulbs and corms and tubers consist of fleshy organs which, when planted, will grow for many seasons.

The classic well-loved combination of the tulip 'China Pink' and forget-me-nots.

PLANT CARE

Weeding the borders in the early part of the year results in much labour saved later on. Where possible the application of a mulch, some form of organic matter, to a depth of about 7.5cm/3in promotes healthy and vigorous plants. Additionally, a mulch reduces water evaporation during dry periods. As flowers develop, a liquid feed may be applied. For this purpose a wide range of fertilizers is available. Manufacturers' instructions should be followed exactly.

As plants begin to grow, those of less robust habit will need some form of staking to protect them from wind and rain. For lower-growing, smaller plants it is sufficient to drive in three or four sticks around

The shrub *Lavatera* 'Burgundy Wine' is visible through an airy haze of *Verbena bonariensis*.

the plant and tie these with string. Hazel or birch twigs are ideal for this. Taller, stronger-growing specimens require a more substantial approach of bamboo canes or manufactured stakes. These should be put in place early in the season; further staking and tying may be necessary at intervals.

Unfortunately, periodically flowers are attacked by pests, virus or fungal disease. The nature and intensity of any attack will vary from season to season. Where diseases are detected at an early stage and treatment carried out, control is relatively easy. In many instances, particularly in the case of pests, Nature herself will take charge. It must be remembered that not all insects are harmful in the garden. Many are not only harmless but helpful.

1. EARLY SPRING

FIRST FLOWERS

PERHAPS NOTHING IS MORE WELCOME in
the garden than the first sightings of
spring flowers to mark the end of the
drab days of winter.

Snowdrops are ideally grown in a woodland situation
although they will prosper in cool, moist soil at the base of
a sunless wall. Here they look splendid in contrast to the
deep red leaves of bergenia.

◆ *Division of snowdrops should take place after flowering but
before the foliage has died down.*

Anemone blanda is a plant for the edge of woodland. Its many petalled blooms are usually of mid-blue. 10 cm/4in

Chionodoxa luciliae The common name, Glory of the Snow, well describes these pretty bluish-lilac flowers. 10cm/4in

Crocus tommasinianus should be placed in drifts in an open position and left undisturbed to naturalize. 10cm/4in

Cyclamen coum is available in many different forms. Leaves are often interestingly marbled. ◑, 10cm/4in

PLANNING AHEAD

Now is the time to order seeds of annuals for summer displays.

Sow half-hardy annuals under glass to plant out when the threat of frost is past.

Hardy annuals may be sown directly into well prepared seed-beds where they are to bloom.

Narcissus cyclamineus is
particularly distinctive with
its protruding trumpet and
reflexed perianth segments.
15–20cm/6–8in

***Narcissus* 'February Gold'**
This miniature daffodil
enjoys damp soil and is an
excellent choice for rough
grass. 15–20cm/6–8in

***Iris reticulata* 'Harmony'**
This blue iris is an early
flowering dwarf form for a
sunny position.
10–15cm/4–6in

◆ *Propagate the
reticulata irises by lifting
and dividing the bulbs in
late summer.*

Iris unguicularis Place the Algerian iris in a pot to stand beside an entrance or doorway for its brief but lovely flowering period. E, ○, 20 × 60cm/ 8in × 2ft

Euphorbia rigida Glaucous leaves make this a most striking spurge. ○, E, 60 × 45cm/1 × 1½ft

It is not simply the range of hues from purest white to deepest black, but the limitless variations of shading, veining and spotting that make *Helleborus orientalis* such magical plants.

Hugging the floor of the woodland, the winter aconite vies with the snowdrop to be amongst the first flowers of spring. Its glossy, bright yellow buttercup flowers will make a splash of gold year after year if left undisturbed. The little blue *Iris histrioides*, 10cm/4in tall, blooms slightly later.

Shade Lovers

Sheets of wood anemone in the wild are one of the delights of springtime.

Primula 'Hose-in-Hose'
Unusual for flowering above
a tiny ruff of leaves.
10 × 10cm/4 × 4in

Vinca minor 'Burgundy' A
coloured form of the lesser
periwinkle in bloom from
mid-spring to autumn.
15 × 60cm+/6in × 2ft+

Anemone apennina The blue flowers of this pretty species
become flattened stars in the spring sun. 10 × 7.5cm/4 × 3in

◆ *Grow erythroniums amongst apennine anemones for a
sparkling carpet of bloom.*

Cardamine trifolia This
delicate little lady's smock
delights with tiny flowers of
pink or white.
20 × 30cm/8in x 1ft

Epimedium × *youngianum*
'Niveum' Small white
flowers are eye-catching in
the early part of the year.
25 × 30cm/10in × 1ft

Anemone nemorosa **'Bowles' Purple'** is one of a number of
cultivated forms of wood anemone. 15 × 30cm/6in × 1ft

◆ *Anemone nemorosa* 'Robinsoniana' *has lavender-blue flowers
and may be more easily obtainable.*

2. SPRING

MASSED EFFECTS

DAFFODILS ANNOUNCE the arrival of spring. Whether in the wild or in the garden their assertive trumpets capture the imagination and bring cheer to the darkest of days.

Narcissus poeticus The pheasant's eye is beautifully scented.
◑ , 45cm/1½ft

◆ *Remove dead heads after flowering but leave foliage to die down.*

***Narcissus* 'Hawera'** Many bulbs are well suited to growing in gravel. Here 'Hawera' enjoys the good drainage. 45cm/1½ft

Muscari neglectum Dense spikes of blue typify the grape hyacinth which is tolerant of most situations. 10–15cm/4–6in

Aubrieta deltoidea A carpeter to spill over walls or paths. Cut back hard after flowering. ○, 5 × 45cm/2in × 1½ft

Myosotis No spring border should be without the much loved forget-me-not. Allow it to seed at will. 15 × 30cm/6in × 1ft

Alyssum saxatile will brighten the rock garden with its yellow flowers. ○, 15 × 30cm/6in × 1ft

Arabis caucasica A profusion of white flowers over evergreen foliage. Good for difficult spots. 15 × 30cm/6in × 1ft

Bulb Care

For spring flowering, plant bulbs during the previous autumn.

As a broad guide bulbs should be planted to at least twice their depth.

Most bulbs may be allowed to remain in the ground although tulips and hyacinths may, if desired, be lifted once the leaves have died down.

An annual dressing of bonemeal lightly forked in before bulbs commence flowering will help to maintain vigour.

Cheiranthus The heady fragrance of wallflowers is one of the many joys of spring. 30 × 30cm/1 × 1ft

A white spring bed dominated by grouped planting of the impressive tulip 'Purissima' with white honesty and primroses.

◆ *Note the effect of repeat plantings of bold subjects.*

SOMETHING UNUSUAL

THE CHOICE OF PLANTS AVAILABLE for
the spring borders is limitless. The
inclusion of something a little
different adds certain style and
transforms the conventional into the
dramatic.

Ipheion uniflorum **'Wisley
Blue'** Starry blue flowers
are an enchanting addition
to the front of the border.
15cm/6in

Erythronium dens-canis is
but one of many dog's tooth
violets enjoying a semi-
shaded, humus rich
situation. 15cm/6in

Pulmonaria **'Bowles' Blue'**
A beautiful lungwort and
one of many available
forms. ◑ , 30 × 45cm/
1 × 1½ft

Dicentra **'Bacchanal'** is an
exceptionally deep red
bleeding heart with finely
cut, glaucous green leaves.
30 × 30cm/1 × 1ft

Fritillaria imperialis The crown imperial is one of the most majestic of garden plants and well worth growing. ○, 1m × 30cm/ 3 × 1ft

In the WILD

THE IMPRESSION of wild flowers
sprinkled amongst gently waving
grasses is something to be desired
and, if possible, copied.

Caltha palustris A good
choice for a damp spot
beside a pond or stream.
◑ , 60 × 60cm/2 × 2ft

Cardamine pratensis The
lady's smock is to be found
growing in damp meadows
and ditches in the wild.
◑ , 25cm/10in

Meconopsis cambrica
Allowed to seed around, the
Welsh poppy will lend a
casual air to the garden.
30 × 30cm/1 × 1ft

Convallaria majalis
Beautifully scented, lily-of-
the-valley will gradually
increase over the years.
◑ , ● , 20cm/8in

Scilla non-scripta Bluebells should mainly be reserved for the wild garden where, left undisturbed, they will naturalize. ◑ , 25cm/10in

Primula **'Valley Red'** Primulas are an attractive addition to the less formal parts of the garden. ◑ , 30 × 30cm/1 × 1ft

Primula vulgaris A cool shady bank makes an ideal site in which to place clumps of primroses. 10cm/4in

3. EARLY
SUMMER

COMBINING PLANTS

AS SUMMER GATHERS PACE so the
borders begin to fill out. Soft, pastel
colours predominate and it is the
arrangement of these which
determines the success or otherwise of
the planting schemes.

A restful arrangement of yellows and blues – delphiniums,
feverfew, salvia, viola and mallow.

SOME ASSOCIATIONS will readily suggest themselves, others will need to be worked at. Teaming copper with lime-green, purple with grey and orange with blue are just a few of the compositions to be tried. Equally successful are blue, white and silver or simply primrose and white.

Aquilegia 'Magpie' A sombre atmosphere is created by placing this unusual aquilegia amongst purple sage. 60 × 45cm/ 2 × 1½ft

◆ *Aquilegias come readily from seed but will frequently cross one with another.*

Erysimum 'Bowles' Mauve'
This perennial wallflower
looks splendid against a
silver background.
60 × 60cm/2 × 2ft

Iris sibirica The lavender
blue of this Siberian flag
tones well with pale pinks.
For moist soil. ◯,
60 × 60cm/2 × 2ft

Lychnis chalcedonica A
difficult red to place outside
a hot scheme. Look out for
the double form.
1m × 45cm/3 × 1½ft

**_Veronica austriaca_ 'Shirley
Blue'** Drift this sprawling
plant throughout a yellow
and blue border. ◯,
20 × 30cm/8in × 1ft

Diascia vigilis Put this pretty
pink with the silver-grey
foliage of lamb's ears _Stachys
byzantina_ 'Silver Carpet'. ◯,
45 × 60cm/1½ x 2ft

Baptisia australis The false
indigo is a worthwhile plant
to seek out and include in a
blue scheme. 75 × 60cm/
2½ × 2ft

BEDDING OUT

RECENT YEARS HAVE SEEN A REVIVAL of formal bedding schemes where massed plants make for eye-catching displays. The large number of plants required can mostly be raised from seed.

Nemesia Easily grown, nemesia is quick to flower in a wide array of colours. ○, 30–45cm/1–1½ft

Limnanthes douglasii (Poached egg flower) Edge a border with this sunny little flower which is loved by bees. ○, 15cm/6in

Salvia splendens There is nothing understated about the many red varieties of this permanently popular annual. ○, 30cm/1ft

Felicia amelloides Plant the blue marguerite in groups to fill any spaces left in sunny borders. ○, 45 × 30cm/1½ × 1ft

Heliotrope Somewhat less commonly used today than in the past, heliotrope (or cherry pie) is strongly perfumed. ○, 45cm/1½ft

Petunia F1 hybrids will give a constant succession of flowers from planting out until the frosts. ○, 15–45cm/6in–1½ft

Pelargonium Zonal pelargoniums are happiest in full sun and make ideal subjects for beds or containers. ○, 45cm/1½ft

◆ *Often commonly named geranium, pelargoniums will not withstand frost.*

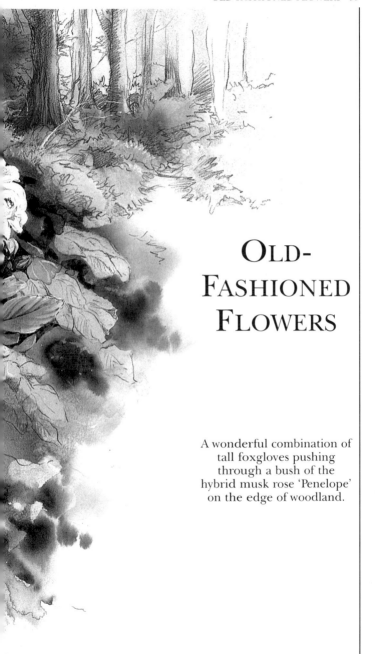

OLD-FASHIONED FLOWERS

A wonderful combination of
tall foxgloves pushing
through a bush of the
hybrid musk rose 'Penelope'
on the edge of woodland.

Polemonium reptans The blue Jacob's ladder will, if left, gently seed around. 30 × 45cm/1 × 1½ft

Hesperis matronalis Although short-lived the scented sweet rocket will usually self-seed. ◐, 75 × 60cm/2½ x 2ft

***Geranium pratense* 'Mrs Kendall Clark'** A charming geranium which fits into many colour schemes. 60 × 60cm/2 x 2ft

Lunaria annua Strictly speaking a biennial, honesty is most often grown for its pearly seed pods. ◐, 75 × 30cm/2½ × 1ft

Aquilegia vulgaris A true cottage-garden plant, the columbine has attractive grey-green leaves. ◐, 75 × 45cm/2½ × 1½ft

Nepeta **'Six Hills Giant'**
Deep blue flowers and
silvery leaves make this a
very attractive plant.
○, 60 × 60cm/2 × 2ft

Rosa gallica **'Camaieux'**
The combination of white,
pink, crimson in this old
rose will excite comment.
1.5 × 1.2m/5 × 4ft

Flag irises enjoy a situation where their creeping
rhizomes can be sun-baked. Here they are shown with
gladiolus.

◆ *Lift irises such as these and divide every few years.*

4. MIDSUMMER

SUMMER SCENTS

MIDSUMMER AIR is perfumed with bewitching scents carried on gentle breezes. Bees murmur throughout long, dreamy days and borders are overrun with fragrant blooms.

Dianthus **'Gravetye Gem'**
All the pinks enjoy an open, free draining site.
○, E, 20 × 30cm/8in × 1ft

Dianthus **'Pike's Pink'** A delightful subject for the rock garden or front of border. ○, E, 15 × 15cm/ 6 × 6in

Lilium candidum Heavily scented flowers in purest white make the Madonna lily an outstanding subject. ○, 1.2m/4ft

Lilium **'Uchida'** Charmingly marked. This lily would be equally at home in a container. ○, 1.2m/4ft

***Phlox* 'Fujiyama'** A handsome plant with large heads of pure white which are pleasantly scented.
○, 1m × 75cm/3 × 2½ft

***Phlox* 'Norah Leigh'** Lilac flowers are carried above prettily variegated leaves.
○, 75 × 60cm/2½ × 2ft

***Hemerocallis lilioasphodelus* (H. flava)** This day lily is scented. Removal of dead heads prolongs flowering.
75 × 75cm/2½ × 2½ft

Lathyrus odoratus is the original sweet pea. Over the years the range of colours has greatly increased.
○, 30cm–2.4m/1–8ft

CONTINUITY OF BLOOM

As the season progresses early-flowering plants, including many of the spring bulbs, will have finished blooming and have died down. To achieve continuity and a well furnished look, these gaps must be filled. In many cases the later-flowering perennials will reach maturity to obscure vacant spaces. Additionally annuals, such as centaurea, clarkia and the deliciously scented stocks, mathiola, can be introduced. These will flower right up until the first of the winter frosts.

Nicotiana The enticing fragrance of
tobacco plants will fill an enclosed space.
○, 30–90 × 30–45cm/1–3 × 1–1½ft

Lavandula No garden should be without generous clumps
of sweet-smelling lavender. ○, 60 × 60cm+/2 × 2ft+

◆ *Clip lavenders hard back in the spring to retain healthy,*
vigorous plants.

A LIVING TAPESTRY

SUCCESSFUL FLOWER DISPLAYS are the
result of much thought and effort.
Combinations are carefully considered
and awareness is given to leaf form as
well as to the colour of individual
blooms.

Linum narbonense settles
happily amongst the paving
stones where its roots enjoy
a cool run. ○, 45 × 30cm/
1½ × 1ft

Monarda didyma '**Croftway
Pink**' (Bergamot) Seen here
against the violet-blue of
nepeta, to good effect.
1m × 45cm/3 × 1½ft

Geranium sanguineum
striatum at the front of the
border to give a full,
informal effect. 30 × 45cm/
1 × 1½ft

Eryngium variifolium The steely blue flower-heads of this sea-holly are rounded and spiky. ○, 45 × 25cm/ 1½ft × 10in

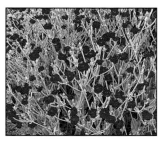

Lychnis coronaria A striking plant although the magenta flowers sometimes make it difficult to place. ○, 45 × 45cm/1½ × 1½ft

Eremurus bungei Conspicuous foxtail lilies dominate plants in a border giving height and interest. ○, 1.5m × 60cm/5 × 2ft

Hemerocallis Clumps of red and orange day lilies convey the full heat of summer in this hot border. 1 × 1m/ 3 × 3ft

***Geranium himalayense* 'Plenum'** Lilac double flowers ensure the popularity of this appealing plant. 60 × 60cm/2 × 2ft

Argyranthemum **'Jamaica Primrose'** A most appealing tender marguerite for a warm spot. ○, 1 × 1m/ 3 × 3ft

Stachys macrantha is distinctive for its purplish-pink flowers. A good front-of-border plant. 45 × 45cm/1½ × 1½ft

Campanula poscharskyana This rockery campanula will quickly spread to cover a wide area. 25 × 60cm/ 10in × 2ft

Campanula pyramidalis A giant Canterbury bell. Plant this to tower through and above old roses. ○, 1.2m × 60cm/4 × 2ft

LOOKING AHEAD

Now is an ideal time in which to plan alterations to the flower garden. A critical look at the borders will show up those plants which perform badly, those which have outgrown their allocated space and those whose colours clash. Intended changes may be noted down in readiness for the autumn when plants may be lifted, divided and moved.

Acanthus spinosissimus Purple-tipped bracts in elegant spikes make this a plant of distinction. ○, 1.2m × 75cm/4 × 2½ft

Geranium psilostemon and *Geranium* **'Johnson's Blue'**
These two hardy geraniums create a dramatic effect when placed together. 60 × 60cm/2 × 2ft

◆ *Bright colours are here toned down with the silver-leafed stachys.*

Lysimachia punctata A colourful border plant but one with a tendency to spread beyond bounds. 75 × 75cm/2½ × 2½ft

Dictamnus albus purpureus Slow to establish but well worth taking trouble over. 60 × 60cm/2 × 2ft

TENDER PERENNIALS

AMONGST THE LOVELIEST and most desirable of summer flowers are those which will not withstand frost. Less-hardy plants make excellent subjects for pots and containers. Grouped together on a terrace or beside a door they can form an attractive feature. Brugmansias, cannas and a phormium dominate this display.

Brugmansia (Angel's trumpet, datura) An excellent plant for a pot. Here, the long, white hanging trumpets look coolly elegant. ○, 1.2 x 1m/4 x 3ft

Lobelia syphilitica These
elegant blue spires would
enhance most situations.
Soil should be kept moist.
1.2m × 30cm/4 × 1ft

Lobelia tupa Spectacular in
flower. This lobelia requires
really good drainage and
protection from winter wet.
○, 1.2m × 30cm/4 × 1ft

Gladiolus **hybrid** Possibly
these tall, rather stiff flower
spikes are at their best in a
formal bedding scheme.
○, 1.2m × 30cm/4 × 1ft

Salvia discolor Absolutely
outstanding. Indigo-black
flowers above white-felted
leaves. Keep frost free. ○,
60 × 30cm/2 × 1ft

COMBAT COLD

Many of these tender perennials will survive the winter provided they are given a frost-free place. Grow them in pots throughout the colder months and then transfer to the open ground for the gardening season. Repot as the temperature falls.

Gazania South African daisies, available in a whole range of colours, make for an intense show.
◯, 30 × 20cm/1ft × 8in

Lobelia cardinalis **'Queen Victoria'** Deep wine red leaves and stems and intense red flowers dominate this striking plant. ◯, 90 × 30cm/3 × 1ft

◆ *Surprisingly this foliage and flower looks superb when set against orange.*

5. LATE SUMMER/ AUTUMN

A LATE SHOW

AS SUMMER DRAWS TO A CLOSE the
autumn flowers come into their own.
Exciting kniphofias, fiery crocosmias
and late-flowering salvias ensure an
interesting and continuous display.

Crocosmia 'Lucifer', *Dahlia*
'Bishop of Llandaff' Placed
together these two late
flowering plants bring
excitement to the border. ○

◆ *Dahlia tubers should be
lifted in the autumn and stored
in a frost-free place.*

Kniphofia caulescens This striking poker has interesting grey-green, serrated leaves. ○, 1m × 60cm/3 × 2ft

Dahlia 'Grenadier' Tuberous dahlias dress up an end of season border. ○, 60 × 60cm/2 × 2ft.

GLOWING COLOURS typify the time of year. A last rose ('Just Joey'), the flat yellow heads of achillea and generous clumps of crocosmias and dahlias maintain interest throughout the garden. In the foreground the crimson tassels of amaranthus (Love-lies-bleeding) elegantly sweep to the ground.

Macleaya microcarpa Allow
plenty of space for this
dramatic perennial.
2 × 1m/6 × 3ft.

Fuchsia magellanica
'Gracilis Variegata' A
graceful shrub with slender
crimson-purple flowers.
75 × 75cm/2½ × 2½ft.

Anemone hybrida Japanese
anemones have a long
flowering period. 1.5m/5ft.

Liriope muscari Tiny spikes
of violet flowers are
sometimes masked by the
leaves. 30 × 45cm/1 × 1½ft.

Crinum powellii These
beautiful, fragrant flowers
are effective against a sunny
wall. ○, 1m × 60cm/3 × 2ft.

♦ *Crinums are not difficult
to grow but like a rich, well
drained soil.*

***Crocosmia* 'Mount Usher'**
No garden should be
without a selection of these
perennials. ○, 60 × 30cm/
2 × 1ft.

Kirengeshoma palmata A
plant for moist ground
close to water. ◖,
1m × 75cm/3 × 2½ft.

***Agapanthus* 'Loch Hope'**
Amongst the most
magnificent of dark blue
forms of African lily. ○,
1.2m × 75cm/4 × 2½ft.

Aconitum carmichaelii
Roots of Monkshood, or
Wolf's bane, are poisonous.
1.5m × 30cm/5 × 1ft.

DAZZLING DAISIES

DAISY-TYPE FLOWERS dominate the late summer borders together with chrysanthemums and dahlias. These heavily petalled blooms enliven the last days of summer.

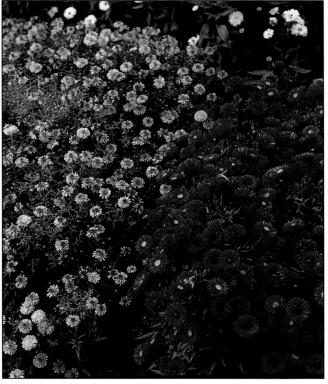

Aster novi-belgii **'Lilac Time'**, *Aster novi-belgii* **'Jenny'** These asters form a pleasing composition. ○

◆ *Taller growing asters require some form of staking. Hazel sticks are ideal.*

***Aster thompsonii* 'Nanus'**
Continuously in flower from mid-summer, this little aster is an invaluable garden plant. 45 × 25cm/1½ft × 10in.

***Aster novi-belgii* 'Goliath'**
Regular division in spring results in freer flowering plants. ○, 1.2m × 45cm/ 4 × 1½ft.

***Aster × frikartii* 'Mönch'** A long flowering period makes this a highly regarded daisy. ○, 75 × 45cm/2½ × 1½ft.

***Aster novi-belgii* 'Beechwood Charm'** Warm, vibrant flowers lighten drear days. ○, 1.2m × 45cm/4 × 1½ft.

***Dendranthema* 'Nathalie'**
Named cultivars are the
result of much crossing and
recrossing. 90cm/3ft.

***Arctotis* × *hybrida* 'Wine'**
Treat this South African
daisy as an annual in colder
areas. ○, 60cm/2ft.

***Dendranthema* 'Ruby
Mound'** Deep ruby red
flowers are tightly packed
together. ○, 1.2m/4ft.

♦ *An effective association is
achieved by planting deep pink
dendranthema with **Sedum
'Autumn Joy'**.*

Rudbeckia fulgida **'Goldsturm'** These prolific yellow daisies with their black central cones seem to last for all time. Dead-heading prolongs the flowering season. ○, 75 × 45cm/ 2½ × 1½ft.

Helianthus **'Monarch'**
Brilliant yellow sunflowers soar skywards above rough foliage. ○, 2.1 × 1m/ 7 × 3ft.

◆ *Grown from seed sunflowers are great favourites with children.*

Schizostylis coccinea
'Sunrise' Kaffir lilies
continue to bloom even in
low temperatures.
60 × 30cm/2 × 1ft

Sedum **'Autumn Joy'**
Butterflies love this sedum
which remains pleasing
throughout the winter.
○, 60 × 60cm/2 × 2ft

LAST BLOOMS

AS THE GARDENING YEAR draws to a close, and thoughts once more turn to spring, there is still much in the flower garden to attract attention and excite interest.

Nerine bowdenii These showy South African bulbs are reliably hardy. ○, 45 × 20cm/1½ft × 8in

◆ *When planting, place bulbs on a little horticultural grit to improve drainage.*

INDEX OF PLANTS